IMAGES
of America

THE MILITARY HISTORY OF BOSTON'S HARBOR ISLANDS

From 1945 to present day, there has been but one gun, or cannon, at Fort Warren on George's Island. Posed on her cannon, in 1975, is Heather Ann Butler (now Mrs. Robert Cook with three children). She is the daughter of the curator of Fort Warren, Gerald W. Butler.

IMAGES
of America

THE MILITARY HISTORY OF BOSTON'S HARBOR ISLANDS

Gerald Butler

ARCADIA
PUBLISHING

ISBN 978-0-7385-0464-3

Published by Arcadia Publishing
Charleston, South Carolina

Printed in the United States of America

Library of Congress Catalog Card Number: 00-104053

For all general information contact Arcadia Publishing at:
Telephone 843-853-2070
Fax 843-853-0044
E-mail sales@arcadiapublishing.com
For customer service and orders:
Toll-Free 1-888-313-2665

Visit us on the Internet at www.arcadiapublishing.com

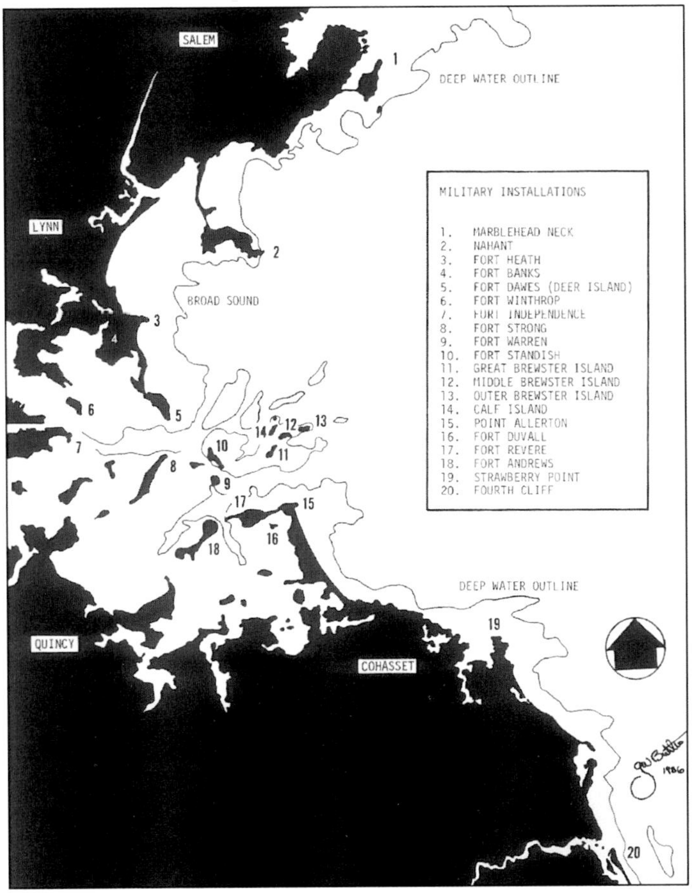

This map shows the military installations of Boston Harbor.

Contents

INTRODUCTION

In May 1632, as part of Governor Winthrop's defense survey, the first earthwork fortification to protect Boston against attack by sea was begun. Located on what was known as Corn Hill (an elevation inland from the present Rowe's Wharf), the fort commanded Boston's inner harbor and passage from the outer harbor. When completed two years later, Corn Hill became known as Fort Hill. In 1687, Governor Andros ordered that the fort be rebuilt and named Fort Andros. This was accomplished, but the structure perished in a spectacular fire in 1760. The stronghold was reworked and occupied by the British during the American Revolution and refortified by General Washington after the war ended, but it served little strategic value. By 1797, the fort was replaced by housing. The area had become a vicious slum by the 1860s, and by 1872, the hill was leveled, most of which was used as fill for the waterfront. By 1979, a parking garage and off-ramp from the Southeastern Expressway to High Street marked the general area.

At the end of the summer of 1634, Governor Winthrop and his advisors recommended and had constructed a fortification on what came to be known as Castle Island. This primitive fort was rebuilt in 1643, but accidentally burned in March 1673. A new fort was quickly constructed in its place and named Fort William and Mary in honor of England's new rulers. In 1701, a new "scientific fortification" of brick was begun and completed by 1703; it later became known as Castle William. Before the American Revolution, the revenue stamps of the hated Stamp Act arrived from England and were stored at Castle William for safety. At the outbreak of the American Revolution, the royal governor of Massachusetts also took refuge in the castle. When British forces evacuated Boston, army engineers blew up the castle. It was immediately rebuilt by the American Army led by Col. Paul Revere. By 1778, the fort on Castle Island was known as Fort Adams. A new fortification was constructed in the early 1800s and President Adams officially named the defensive work Fort Independence. By 1851, a new, granite Fort Independence was constructed and garrisoned.

In 1636, another fort was constructed at the base of Fort Hill; it became known as the Boston Sconce or the South Battery. In 1696, this work was enlarged and became the strongest and most heavily fortified site in the colonies by 1743. The site was in ruins when the British occupied Boston during the American Revolution, and the Americans rebuilt it.

In 1646, the area of Merry's Point was selected to have another fortification constructed around an existing wharf. When completed, this work was named the North Battery. Although rebuilt and enlarged in 1739, the North Battery was in ruins when the British occupied Boston. In the following century, land-filling created two roads in the area—Battery and Salutation Streets—whose names alone give any indication of the existence of the fortification. By 1789, both the south and north batteries were dismantled and sold.

A proposal to defend the port against an enemy fleet equipped with "fireships" was adopted in September 1673. Loaded with inflammable materials, fireships were sailed by skeleton crews close enough to a port or anchored fleet for the ship to drift in on tide and wind; the crew then lit fuses and abandoned the ship. The blazing fireships would lodge against wooden wharves, spreading the fires to the wooden buildings and yards of the waterfront. The only defense against these terror-ships was a barricade or a staggered seawall outlying the immediate port area. Known as the Barricado, this stone defense was completed in 1681. When the threat of fireships passed, the Barricado was put to different use. In 1710, King Street (now known as State Street) was extended out to the center of the Barricado, which formed the original "T" of "T Wharf," and progressed beyond. The last segment of the Barricado was used in the construction of Central Wharf in 1816. The general line of the Barricado is best represented today by Atlantic Avenue.

In the early 1800s, the need for additional seacoast fortifications was noted by American engineers. Overseen by Col. Sylvanus Thayer, the first superintendent of West Point Military Academy, solid granite forts were constructed at Castle Island (Fort Independence), Governor's Island (Fort Winthrop), and George's Island (Fort Warren). All three forts were heavily garrisoned during the War Between the States, but no fort was more strategic than Fort Warren. Known as "the Key to Boston Harbor," Fort Warren received over 1,000 Confederate and political prisoners in addition to its defensive role.

It is at this point in history that *The Military History of Boston's Harbor Islands* begins.

One

Stone Citadels

This construction of a typical pre–Civil War fort shows granite blocks being prepared, rail carts for moving blocks to the construction area, and horses for power. A "gin pole," or derrick, used to move the granite blocks can be seen on the left.

This 1885 photograph of Fort Independence shows the garrison soldiers in formation with rifles and bayonets fixed. In the foreground, four officers can be seen with their swords lowered at

rest. In the background, atop the ramparts, a typical pre– and post–Civil War seacoast cannon can be seen.

To date, this is the only known photograph taken inside Fort Independence during the Civil War. The military unit designs on the parade ground depict Union Army units that served at the fort.

Edgar Allan Poe enshrined Fort Independence in American literature, using material learned during his eight-month service there with Company H of the 1st U.S. Artillery. On May 26, 1827, Poe enlisted under the name Edgar A. Perry at Castle Island. One off-duty summer evening, he heard the legend that had grown up around the fatal Christmas Day duel of Light Artillery Lts. Robert F. Massie and Gustavus Drane, 1817. Massie, a popular fellow, and Drane, a disagreeable character, had quarreled on Christmas Eve. Fueled by alcohol, the quarrel escalated into a duel the following dawn. Accompanied by their seconds, Massie and Drane chose their weapons and fought a short distance from the fort's main gate. Massie was mortally wounded. Neither of the seconds would testify against Drane and he was transferred. Massie's fellow officers subscribed for a memorial obelisk which is now placed at Fort Devens, Devens, Massachusetts.

In the legend, a group of officers and trusted enlisted men deal out a different justice to the nameless and disfavored victor of the duel. Feigning friendship, officers and men take turns getting the duelist insensibly intoxicated and wall him up alive in an unused niche deep within the fort. Private Poe captured the terror of this legend in "The Cask of Amontillado," first published in *Godey's Lady's Book* in November 1846. (Drawing by Gerald Butler.)

In 1884, a group of 13th Massachusetts Regiment Civil War veterans who had served at Fort Independence during the early summer of 1861 returned for a reunion. Here, six of them are seen outside the main entrance of the fort.

In this photograph, the same group of veterans are seen inside the fort, displaying a sign that proclaims this is where they were quartered during the early summer of 1861.

This remarkable view of Fort Winthrop on Governor's Island in the late 19th century was taken from atop Fort Independence. In the center of the island the huge granite "keep" of Fort Winthrop can be seen. This area is now one of Logan International Airport's busiest runways.

This view of Fort Winthrop's parapet shows a Rodman smoothbore cannon on its carriage. Adjacent are two unmounted cannon tubes, minus carriages. The weapons were probably never mounted at Fort Winthrop.

The entrance to Fort Warren on George's Island appears in this 1865 Civil War view. Photographed from near the wharf, the guardhouse and sentry box can easily be seen in the background. The side of the granite fort (Bastion D) visible is the location of the Civil War Hospital.

Although not photographed during the Civil War, this late-19th-century photograph taken from the wharf shows the massiveness of the fort as well as the beautiful granite architecture designed by Col. Sylvanus Thayer.

This Civil War era photograph shows a formal view of the entrance to Fort Warren and its guardhouse. The earth ramp in the background led to the bridge (behind the sentry and sentry box) that, in turn, went over the dry moat and into the sallyport, or main entrance of the fort proper. The sallyport was protected by a drawbridge, which, when raised, lowered a Portcullis (gate) that effectively sealed-off the fort against invaders.

One of the finest Civil War views of Fort Warren, this March 1864 photograph shows a formal formation and review of Union troops on the parade ground. Most of the fort's guns have not been

mounted and the ramparts are mostly vacant. The background area—where the three flights of stairs are visible—is Bastion B. This is the area of the fort purportedly visited by the Black Widow.

Although not taken during the Civil War, this photograph of the interior of Fort Warren shows the tremendous amount of armament mounted at the fort. Seen is the area between Bastion B (right) and Bastion C (left). The small opening is the "postern" entrance that led to the outer

batteries of the island. Coincidentally, this is the same area where enlisted Confederate soldiers and sailors were incarcerated.

This exterior view of enlisted men's quarters shows a covered entrance with benches set under it for the men to smoke their off-duty and evening pipes. This area of the fort was later modified to house powerful 12-inch disappearing rifles at the top, while the quarters below became ammunition and support areas. Notice the blanket pylons outside each casemate entrance and the fresh water pump to the right.

Conditions for the enlisted men were not all that bad after the Civil War. Shown is a typical casemate room with bunks, stove, table, and chairs. A rifle rack can be seen adjacent to the stove, while uniforms and equipment are located on a shelf over each soldier's bunk. The three windows were originally musketry loopholes from which riflemen could fire into the dry moat if the fort was under siege. The loopholes were widened in the late 1800s to improve air circulation.

This grim, posed assemblage of Confederate States of America prisoners of war were incarcerated at Fort Warren during April 1864. This group, located outside their casemate room, were enlisted soldiers and sailors. Most of the sailors were from the C.S.S. *Atlanta* and C.S.S. *Tacony*. Between 35 to 45 men were contained within a single casemate room in three-tiered bunks, while meals and cooking were effected by a large pot outside the chamber.

Officers and political prisoners fared much better than the enlisted men. Although conditions were sometimes crowded, Fort Warren was considered a very humane prisoner of war camp.

The most famous prisoner of war at Fort Warren was the vice president of the Confederacy Alexander H. Stephens. After Gen. Robert E. Lee surrendered on April 9, 1865, Alexander H. Stephens and John H. Reagen (respectively, the vice president and the postmaster general of the Confederate states) were captured and sent to Fort Warren. Facing possible execution, the two men were confined in separate casemates and forbidden to "communicate with each other, or with any other person, either verbally or in writing."

Alexander Stephens amused himself by purchasing a small thermometer. By opening and closing windows in his casemate chamber, he kept the temperature at a constant level. On October 14, 1865, Stephens and Reagen were pardoned and released; they departed the island on the afternoon boat.

Two

MODERNIZATION

Post–Civil War modifications of Fort Independence, begun in 1871 and completed in 1876, included additional magazines, more gun platforms, and protection for the gun crews. Fort Independence was abandoned by the U.S. Army in 1880. In May 1890, Castle Island was given back to the City of Boston to be used as a park, except Fort Independence, which remained under federal control. The fort was regarrisoned during the War of 1898 and used as an important submarine mine depot.

Advances in weapons technology during the Civil War and the experience gained from naval attacks against fortifications led to improvements in the forts defending Boston Harbor throughout the 1870s. Accelerating progress in metallurgy, explosives, ballistics, and communications in the 1880s created long-range, breech-loading artillery of increased accuracy and destructive power. Emplaced on land or carried in heavily armored, steam-powered warships, the new guns led to an international arms race that still goes on today.

By 1885, the U.S. War Department Board on Fortifications (the Endicott Board) began designing harbor fortifications constructed of a new material, reinforced concrete, that would be located further from the port cities they protected. While these new fortifications were in the process of construction, older guns and systems were modified, as shown in this image of a gun battery at Fort Warren during the War of 1898.

In 1891, construction of an emplacement for one 8-inch gun (later a 10-inch) mounted on a revolutionary disappearing carriage was begun in Bastion B of Fort Warren. A scientific article of the period claimed, "The disappearing gun is visible above the parapet only for a few seconds as it rises to fire, and, if smokeless powder is used, all that can be seen is a momentary black spot among the green slopes in which the battery is hidden."

The 12-inch gun tubes for Battery Stevenson are manhandled in this 1902 photograph. The old Civil War guardhouse can be seen to the left while the modern guardhouse is at the center and right of this image.

This 1910 photograph shows the proud Coast Artillery Corps Band of Boston Harbor prior to a martial review held at Fort Warren. In the background, Bastion B and the first disappearing gun battery in Boston Harbor, Battery Jack Adams, can be seen.

Another view of Fort Warren's Bastion B shows a 1910 battalion review of the Massachusetts Volunteer Militia, later known as the Massachusetts National Guard. In this image, from left to right, are the mine observation station and rapid-fire gun emplacement (Battery Plunkett) on Bastion B, Battery Adams, and Battery Stevenson's massive emplacement of two 12-inch disappearing guns.

Although used as an artillery site during the Revolutionary and Civil Wars, Long Island was not acquired by the federal government until 1867. By 1899, five emplacements for 10-inch disappearing guns (Batteries Hitchcock and Ward) and a 4.7-inch quick-firing emplacement (Battery Drum) were completed. By 1906, four rapid-fire gun emplacements along the water's edge (Batteries Basinger, Stevens, Smyth, and Taylor) were finished. The island defense site became designated Fort Strong.

This image of Fort Strong was taken from the opposite vantage point as that of the above photograph. Visible are Long Island Lighthouse to the left, the mine support buildings below, and the line of gun batteries along the top. The small building to the rear of the gun batteries is an observation station.

A 60-inch searchlight (No. 12) is in its shelter at Fort Strong. The searchlight lens reflects inside its shelter, while the Long Island Lighthouse can be seen atop the hill. This light swept the main channel toward Deer Island.

A 60-inch searchlight (No. 11) appears in its operating or nighttime position at Fort Strong. During the daytime, the searchlight was housed in the shelter for concealment and protection. This light was mounted above the seawall at the tip of Fort Strong to sweep the outer harbor area when required.

Lovell's Island, once used for decoy camps and gun batteries by the French during the Revolutionary War, was proposed for a series of iron turrets and dynamite guns in the late 1800s. By 1900, the island became designated Fort Standish and boasted seven coastal defense batteries of varying calibers as well as a multitude of supportive systems. Shown are two gun crew members at the breech of a 10-inch gun.

The island had many fire-control structures, such as observation stations, searchlights, and power plants. Shown is the power plant for the 60-inch searchlight. In this building were located powerful gasoline engines that provided power for the searchlights and ancillary systems on the island when connected to electrical generators. This structure remains on Fort Standish today, although overgrown and vandalized.

The largest of the Fort Standish arsenal were the four 10-inch guns mounted on disappearing carriages (Battery Burbeck-Morris). In this photograph, one of the guns is shown ready to fire in the raised, or firing, position. Notice the soldier at the rear of the gun tube.

This remarkable photograph shows Battery Burbeck-Morris firing. In most instances, smokeless powder was used to insure that an enemy fleet would not spot the billows of smoke as a gun fired, as can be seen in this somewhat obscured image. Other gun batteries on Fort Standish included three 6-inch disappearing guns (Battery Terrill), two 6-inch guns on barbette carriages (Battery Whipple), and three 3-inch rapid-fire gun batteries (Batteries Williams, Weir, and Vincent).

By 1897, the U.S. War Department had acquired the necessary land on Peddock's Island for a seacoast fortification installation, and construction for a massive eight mortar long-range battery began. Four mortars were established in open protected pits with ammunition and plotting rooms underground. Shortly thereafter, the site was designated Fort Andrews. The first mortar battery was completed in 1901 (Battery Whitman) and a second unit was immediately commenced. Completed in 1904, this unit was also an eight mortar unit (Battery Cushing). Here, squad tents line the main road of Fort Andrews mortar battery.

A two gun, 6-inch barbette emplacement (Battery McCook) and two rapid-fire gun batteries of four guns (Batteries Rice and Bumpus) were completed in 1904. In this photograph, Battery McCook is shown, while Battery Bumpus can be seen on the far right.

Telegraph Hill, in Hull, was fortified during the Revolutionary War and chosen for seacoast fortifications through the late 1800s. (For further information, see *Images of America: Hull and Nantasket Beach.*) In 1900, the site was designated Fort Revere; by 1906, multiple gun batteries and observation stations had been constructed. The largest of these stations included two 12-inch guns in barbette (Battery Ripley), six 6-inch guns on disappearing carriages (Batteries Pope and Sanders), and two 5-inch guns on barbette mounts (Battery Field). Battery Ripley is shown with its unique rear loading platform.

This view of Officer's Row, Fort Revere, was taken from Battery Ripley. The water tower (standpipe) is in the upper center of image, and three permanent officer's quarters can be seen along the road below. The center building is now the Fort Revere museum and visitor's center.

A second series of emplacements for long-range mortars proposed for the North Shore of Boston was eventually placed in central Winthrop. The construction began in 1891 for two separate batteries of 12-inch mortars. Both installations were completed by 1896 and consisted of two pits of four mortars each (Batteries Lincoln and Kellogg). Shown is the proof-firing of one of the 12-inch mortars in 1898.

This pit, or detail, view shows the powerful 12-inch mortars established at Fort Banks. Additional buildings, fire control, and barracks were completed in 1898; the reservation was designated Fort Banks.

The Fort Banks mortar batteries were initially selected to be established at Grover's Cliff in Winthrop. Final engineering studies eliminated the mortar battery, but created a 12-inch gun battery in its place. The land was acquired by 1895; by 1901, the three 12-inch guns, mounted on disappearing carriages, were completed (Battery Winthrop). The site, with searchlight and observation stations, became designated Fort Heath.

This 12-inch gun on Battery Winthrop shows the massiveness and complexity of the disappearing carriage.

Since the early 1880s, Deer Island was recommended to have fortifications and observation stations. In 1898, the federal government acquired the island for range and direction finding stations. By 1907, a series of fire-control and mine observation stations were constructed at the north and south ends of the island.

By 1913, two 60-inch searchlights were established at the northern and southern limits of Deer Island. This image shows the northern 60-inch searchlight in its operating position. The protected shelter for the light was located to the rear and required a powerful winch to bring the light, mounted on a small rail cart, to either operating or sheltered positions.

During the war of 1898, Bayley's Hill, located in the North Shore town of Nahant, served as an important observation, range-finding, and field artillery station. In 1902, land was purchased by the U.S. War Department for mortar batteries. By 1907, a permanent observation station had been established at the location shown above. The powerful mortars were never established at the site, and the project was terminated in July 1918.

The unique, cliff-mounted 60-inch searchlight in Bayley's Hill, Nahant is shown in its extended, or operating, position over the cliff's edge. The concrete shelter is visible at right.

Three

WORLD WAR I

Fort Independence was used as an observation station by both army and navy personnel during World War I. Two circular, concrete anti-aircraft gun blocks were constructed atop the fort, but no guns were ever mounted. It was used for the storage of small arms ammunition and ordnance. Immediately following the war, the island was used as a park again, except for Fort Independence, which still remained under federal control. In this postwar image, a cannon outside the fort is used by South Boston young men as a vantage point to view incoming and outgoing shipping in Boston Harbor.

In 1917, Fort Warren was the headquarters for the Coast Defenses of Boston Harbor. Fort Warren's importance as Southern Mine Command (Nantasket Roads and the Narrows) increased. Mines and submarine nets were planted in early April 1917, and Boston Harbor was effectively sealed from German submarines. In this image, Fort Warren's mine area and wharf are seen with the post hospital and barracks to the left.

During the war, numerous soldiers trained at Fort Warren while processing to go overseas with artillery units such as the famous 55th Coast Artillery Regiment. In this photograph, taken from the post hospital, the main barracks at Fort Warren are shown. At this location, many of the new recruits were processed into the military.

Mine planting operations in the Southern Mine Group area (Nantasket Roads and the Narrows) were located between George's Island and Hull and Lovell's Island, respectively. The all-purpose M boat is shown in the minefield, while a spotting staff is raised to locate the mine's position for mine observation stations at Forts Warren and Strong.

Army mine planting operations in the Southern Mine Group area show an L boat (L-52) as it prepares to plant a distribution box onto the seabed of the minefield. This unit, later called a selector box, connected electrically and could activate individual mines in the minefield from a mine casemate at Fort Warren.

These photographs show the U.S. Army Mine Planter *Absalom Baird* in the Southern Mine Group in process of planting a minefield. The object alongside the craft is a mine marker buoy and is seen being lowered into the minefield proper. The large reel at the bow of the mine planter contains underwater cables that connect the mines to the distribution boxes and to the mine casemate at Fort Warren.

Fort Strong was the mine center for the Northern Mine Group during WWI responsible for President Roads, the main shipping channel of Boston Harbor. The northern group used systems and equipment identical to those at Fort Warren. Fort Strong was also used as a training site for soldiers processing for overseas units. A militia (now a national guard) soldier is shown after setting up his tent at Fort Strong in 1917.

Soldiers at Fort Strong practice artillery drill on the 10-inch disappearing guns of Battery Hitchcock-Ward in 1917. Each projectile was manually rammed into the breech by the gun crew, as is shown in this image.

Fort Standish on Lovell's Island was also used as a training facility during WWI. The island lacked the comfort that the larger island forts offered, as evidenced by this 1917 view of post headquarters. Personnel stationed on this island lived in tents year-round, which proved to be a great hardship during the severe winter of 1918.

Observation and fire-control (accurate gun-laying) were absolutely essential for the massive guns at Fort Standish and other harbor forts. In this image, the officer of the day peers out from one of the observation stations on the island in spring 1918.

Fort Andrews on Peddock's Island shared the responsibility of training soldiers and processing them for overseas duty during WWI. In this photograph, coast artillery personnel from the 55th Coast Artillery Regiment are seen in formation on the parade grounds.

Coast artillery soldiers in formation and drill at Fort Andrews. In the background are the permanent brick barracks. To the right is the reservation wharf and landing.

Fort Revere also shared the responsibility of troop processing and training during WWI. Armaments were removed for shipment overseas; by late 1917, only two gun batteries—Battery Ripley and Battery Sanders—remained operational. In this image, a long temporary wooden barrack can be seen directly behind Battery Ripley.

This photograph of Fort Revere was taken from behind Battery Ripley. Officer's Row can be seen in the background while the observation station is visible in the lower right corner. Adjacent to the observation station are the permanent barracks and guardhouse.

Ideally located in central Winthrop with railroad lines near the facility, Fort Banks became a major processing and training facility during WWI. The severe winter of 1917–1918 was offset by the kindness of the townspeople of Winthrop who provided the soldiers with extra blankets and home-cooked pastries and pies. In this image, Fort Banks noncommissioned officers of the training cadre line up after artillery drill.

The Fort Banks 12-inch mortars were maintained constantly by garrison soldiers and new trainees. Shortly after the war, the two mortar batteries were modified by removal of four mortars, two from each battery.

This front view of the Fort Banks guardhouse was photographed from the main road. Inside the deceptive building were standard jail cells and chambers for the personnel on guard duty and the officer of the day.

In 1922, the headquarters for the Coast Defenses of Boston transferred from Fort Warren to Fort Banks. It then became known as the Harbor Defenses of Boston and was located in this wooden building on the main road at Fort Banks.

During WWI, the observation station and searchlight at Bayley's Hill in Nahant, were in constant use. Temporary barracks and buildings were quickly constructed for the soldiers manning the facilities, as this photograph taken from Colby Hill shows. Shortly after the war ended, the military reservation at Nahant was designated Fort Ruckman.

Begun during WWI, the Nahant Gun Battery consisted of two long-range 12-inch guns mounted on revolutionary high-angle barbette carriages. When completed in 1923, the battery was designated Battery Gardner. This image shows gun No. 1 of Battery Gardner as seen from the caretaker's cottage that was erected later.

A segment of Sen. Henry Cabot Lodge's estate was used as a searchlight station for the duration of WWI. A powerful 60-inch searchlight was installed near the tip of East Point, Nahant, and maintained a wide sweep of illumination from Marblehead Neck to Deer Island. After the war, the equipment was removed; by 1919, not a vestige of the searchlight station remained.

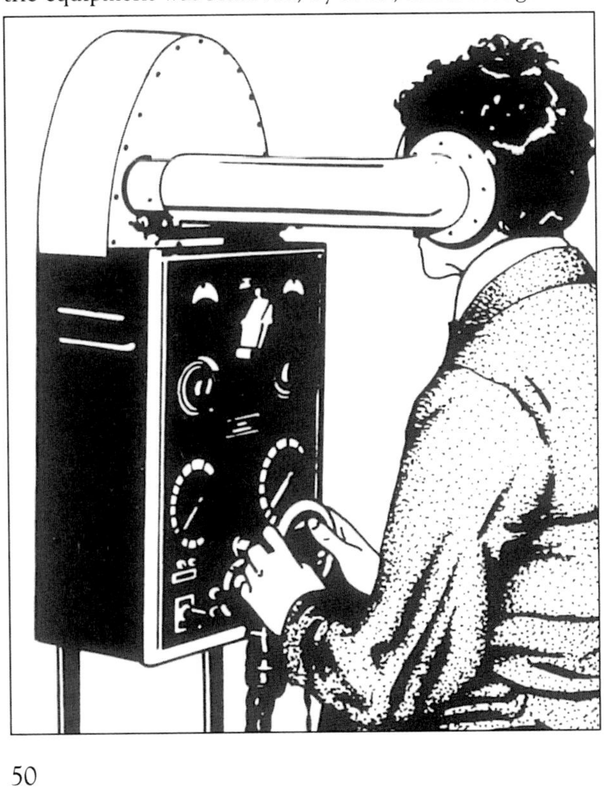

In 1917, the U.S. Navy, with civilian contractors, established a secret laboratory to detect submarines at East Point, Nahant. Chosen for its strategic location and surrounding deep water, the site was ideally remote yet accessible. The secret site was designated the Nahant Antisubmarine Laboratory, and within a short time, scientists created a submarine detector that operated on principles of subaqueous sound detection and could detect submarines at great distances. The laboratory was terminated after the war.

Four

Maintenance Status

In the late 1920s, Castle Island was connected to the mainland by a filled walkway. In 1932, a new roadway, now known as William J. Day Boulevard, was opened with a large traffic rotary in sight of the fort. In 1939, the U.S. Army closed off Castle Island again; sentinels patrolled the radio station, and trucks periodically unloaded small arms ammunition inside the granite fort. In this image, the United States Lines S.S. *Leviathan* is shown from Castle Island in 1930.

In 1930, a plan to extend the runways of Boston Airport, now Logan International Airport, over Governor's Island gained considerable support. Deteriorating Fort Winthrop fell prey to vandals and thrill seekers: graffiti adorned the granite fortifications and, in warmer months, brush fires were frequent. In this 1939 view, the full extent of vandalism can be seen within the main chambers of the fort.

In 1940, Governor's Island was proposed for the storage of munitions being shipped to Great Britain as part of the Lend-Lease Act. This possibility was eliminated because of the proximity of the airport and the possibility that the island might soon be connected to the airport's runway system. This *c.* 1939 view shows the empty exterior parapets.

This view of Fort Warren from the Narrows shows the channel between George's Island and Lovell's Island. The post hospital and wharf can be seen on the left of this 1938 photograph.

On June 9, 1935, Comdr. Charles Robinson of the Grand Army of the Republic and William B. Newell, representing Confederate veterans, unveiled a tablet in the Fort Warren casemate where James Murray Mason and John Slidell, Confederate envoys to Great Britain, and the vice president of the Confederacy Alexander H. Stephens had been incarcerated during the Civil War. The chamber (Casemate Room 7) became a memorial to all Confederate prisoners held at the fort and a library for the garrison.

By the mid-1920s, all of the temporary WWI buildings on Long Island had been demolished. In 1935, Fort Strong's antiaircraft gun battery was modified to include three guns. In successive years, modifications to the mine system and structures took place. In this 1938 aerial view, the Long Island Hospital is in the foreground and Fort Strong is beyond. Officer's Row is in the center of the photograph.

These 1938 photographs show artillery drill on the 10-inch disappearing guns at Fort Strong. The coast artillerymen, called "cosmoliners" or "concrete soldiers," are from the 9th Coast Artillery Regiment headquartered at Fort Banks in central Winthrop.

Fort Standish on Lovell's Island became known as the sandspit early in its military occupation, and the nickname carried through World War II. New fortification structures and observation stations were constructed during the 1920s on the island, while some of the older gun batteries were disarmed. The above image shows a government transport boat bringing supplies to Fort Standish in 1934.

Soldiers at Fort Standish practice artillery drill on one of the 3-inch antiaircraft guns in 1938. At that time, modifications to the antiaircraft guns had taken place and the fort boasted three new antiaircraft guns in operation.

Although Fort Andrews on Peddock's Island was on maintenance status by 1923, construction and modernization of existing and new systems continued. New observation and range-finding stations were built, including this unique 60-inch disappearing searchlight unit that was only raised from its below ground shelter when in operation.

The most modern mortars in the U.S. Army's Coast Artillery Corps were installed at Fort Andrews. In this image, a model M1908 12-inch mortar of Battery Whitman is shown.

Shortly after WWI, Fort Revere's temporary buildings and barracks were demolished and the fort was relegated to maintenance status. During the early 1920s, the fort received modernization that included a 60-inch disappearing searchlight, new observation stations, and range-finding structures.

The unique 36-inch searchlight, mounted on the observation deck of the Fort Revere standpipe, was declared obsolete and removed by 1929. By 1936, three new 3-inch antiaircraft guns had been mounted as part of Boston Harbor's antiaircraft defenses.

The above image shows the Fort Revere standpipe as it looked in 1938; it remains relatively unchanged today.

Coast artillery personnel from Headquarters Battery and line Batteries A and C, 9th Coast Artillery Regiment, garrisoned Fort Banks through WWII. In this image, a formal inspection under arms is being conducted at the fort in 1938.

In addition to coast artillery responsibilities and duties, Fort Banks soldiers were also required to be fully qualified infantrymen and were drilled and inspected regularly. In this photograph, members of Battery A, 9th Coast Artillery Regiment, prepare for a Saturday morning full field inspection.

This view of Fort Heath shows Battery Winthrop and the caretaker's automobile under a heavy snow covering in 1938. Fort Heath was reduced to maintenance status shortly after WWI, but in 1933, the U.S. Navy built and operated a radio direction finder station (RDF) with three tall aerial masts.

In the mid-1920s, a number of concrete observation stations assigned to Winthrop's gun and mortar batteries were built on Deer Island. Additionally, mine observation and range-finding stations were constructed. The U.S. Navy operated an RDF station from the island. In 1939, a modern seawards defense station, H station, was established and tactically controlled Boston Harbor. This aerial view of Deer Island in 1939 shows most of the structures on the reservation.

Fort Ruckman in Nahant conducted experiments using observation balloons for aerial observation and gun-laying in the early 1920s through 1925. These images shows a U.S. Army winch truck and soldiers assigned to these experiments.

Hog Island, located behind Point Allerton and one-half mile southeast of Fort Revere, was acquired by the federal government in 1917 for long-range 12-inch guns. The underground emplacement was identical to Battery Gardner in Nahant. By the early 1920s, the battery was adapted for powerful 16-inch guns of the latest manufacture. These two images show varying phases of construction at the massive gun battery.

In 1922, Hog Island became designated Fort Duvall and the completed 16-inch gun battery Battery Long. In these images, members of Battery A, 9th Coast Artillery Regiment, perform maintenance on the gigantic carriages and guns of Battery Long.

Members of the 9th Coast Artillery Regiment clean the gun tube of gun No. 1 at Battery Long in 1938. The massiveness and complexity of the gun tube and carriage is clearly shown in comparison with the soldier to the left of the carriage.

This interior view of the Battery Long power plant was photographed immediately following installation of the General Electric Company manufactured 25 kilowatt gasoline engines and generator sets. Notice the civilian engineer and inspector from General Electric Company in the background.

Five

World War II

Fort Independence, Fort Warren, Fort Strong, Fort Standish, Fort Andrews

In September 1940, military police took over the guardianship of Fort Independence. The old granite fort was going to be used as a small arms ammunition storage area once again. A small wooden barrack was constructed next to the fort for the military police contingency, and the entire area was restricted to all but military personnel. A high-explosive ammunition depot was scheduled for the stretch of land along the island's causeway and harbor's edge. Shown is one of the last groups to visit the fort in 1940.

Shortly after the official entry of the United States into WWII, British and American scientists, working for the U.S. Navy, began a secret research project at Fort Independence. With headquarters located at Pier II of the Boston Naval Shipyard, the scientists studied the magnetic properties of ships in an attempt to defeat German magnetic mines and torpedoes.

The navy established the facility that officially became the Castle Island Degaussing Station in January 1942. A wooden two-story cottage constructed atop Bastion C of Fort Independence contained the degaussing station's electronic equipment and an observation bridge to signal ships.

The Castle Island degaussing facility consisted of instruments that measured changes that a vessel exhibits in the earth's magnetic field. A magnetometer proving ground was also established at the site that allowed a moored ship to be measured magnetically. In January 1943, a secret "deperming" system was introduced at the facility and was located off the southeast side of Fort Independence. This highly classified operation used special barges, arrays of electronics, and a 900-foot wooden pier for its systems.

In September 1940, Federalized Massachusetts National Guard soldiers once again garrisoned Fort Warren. This unit, the 241st Coast Artillery Regiment, garrisoned most of the Boston Harbor forts and supported the regular army personnel, the 9th Coast Artillery Regiment. Both regiments were in the process of being brought up to full strength. Above, officers of the 241st Coast Artillery Regiment pose at Fort Warren.

Temporary wooden buildings soon covered Fort Warren's landscape, while the old casemated quarters in the granite fort were reconditioned for the new soldiers. An aerial view of Fort Warren, taken in June 1944, shows the military-occupied area of the island.

While modernized and new gun emplacements were under construction, the older weapons of Fort Warren were kept at the ready. In this view, one of the 12-inch disappearing guns of Battery Stevenson is being maintained and drilled upon by its gun crew in 1942.

The nerve center of the gun battery was the plotting room. This 1942 photograph shows the plotting room of Battery Stevenson and shows personnel who were designated "range rats" by the gun crew. The personnel manned telephones from distant observation stations and the plotting board upon which the target is tracked.

This winter 1944 blizzard view shows the post hospital (right) and a temporary wooden mess hall (left) in the northern area of Fort Warren.

Two areas outside the granite fort were designated for quarters and administration. This image shows the northern area under winter 1944 conditions. In the background, Fort Standish is to the right and Gallup's Island is to the left.

The most important function at Fort Warren was the mine command during WWII. The mine casemate at Fort Warren controlled the mines in the southern channel of Boston Harbor (Nantasket Roads). In this photograph, the mine casemate is being sandbagged for protection against shell or shrapnel splinters.

These ground mine panel boards were located in the Fort Warren mine casemate in 1944. All of the ground mines in the southern channel of Boston Harbor could be activated from these panels when required. To eliminate misfiring, a mine required 440 volts to be detonated.

In late June 1942, a disturbance in the outer minefield in Nantasket Roads alerted the evening operator at the Fort Warren mine casemate. His emergency call to the Harbor Entrance Control Post at Fort Dawes brought the entire harbor defense system to full alert. Searchlights and gun batteries swept the sea surface, but no vessels were seen. First Naval District Intelligence immediately reported that no Allied shipping or submarines were within 200 miles of Boston Harbor.

It became apparent to the mine casemate operators that a submerged craft was maneuvering through the newly planted minefield. As the craft turned through the final line of mines, its propeller slashed into a mine casing, thus allowing seawater to enter and ground the mine. The mines were not set to detonate on contact at this time. Before the order could be issued to activate another mine, the undersea intruder reversed course and retraced its route back out of the minefield—an enviable example of seamanship.

The ovoid mine struck by the undersea intruder rests near the Fort Warren wharf. The chalk lines indicate where the mine had been spun during the propeller contact.

The mine command at Fort Warren was completely modernized mid-WWII. In this view, a new L boat (L-91) is seen with cabling running to a distribution box prior to its planting.

The U.S. Army Mine Planter *Abbott* tied up to the Fort Warren wharf in 1943. The ovoid objects to the left of the wharf are the buoyant mines. These were later replaced by the modern ground mine that have a conical appearance.

This view aboard the mine planter *Abbott* shows final preparation before lowering a ground mine onto the seabed. The plucky soldier atop the mine must manually pull the release to lower the mine to the seabed.

Cabling aboard the deck of the mine planter *Abbott* can be seen prior to lowering the last ground mine in a line of mines. Notice the multitude of reels, cables, winches, davits, and mechanical devices required for this operation.

Located on top of Bastion C of the old granite fort at Fort Warren was the H station or the sub-signal station of the Harbor Entrance Control Post. This brick structure remains in place at present and offers an ideal vantage point of Boston Harbor.

During the war, the sergeants at Fort Warren spent what little off-duty time existed at the NCO Club. This refurbished room was the former post bakery during the Civil War.

This 1942 water view shows Fort Strong on Long Island. The mine command area is in the center of this photograph, while Long Island Head is to the left.

Off-duty soldiers from Battery A, 9th Coast Artillery Regiment at Fort Strong relax in a late afternoon pose. In the front row of soldiers is the battery's mascot.

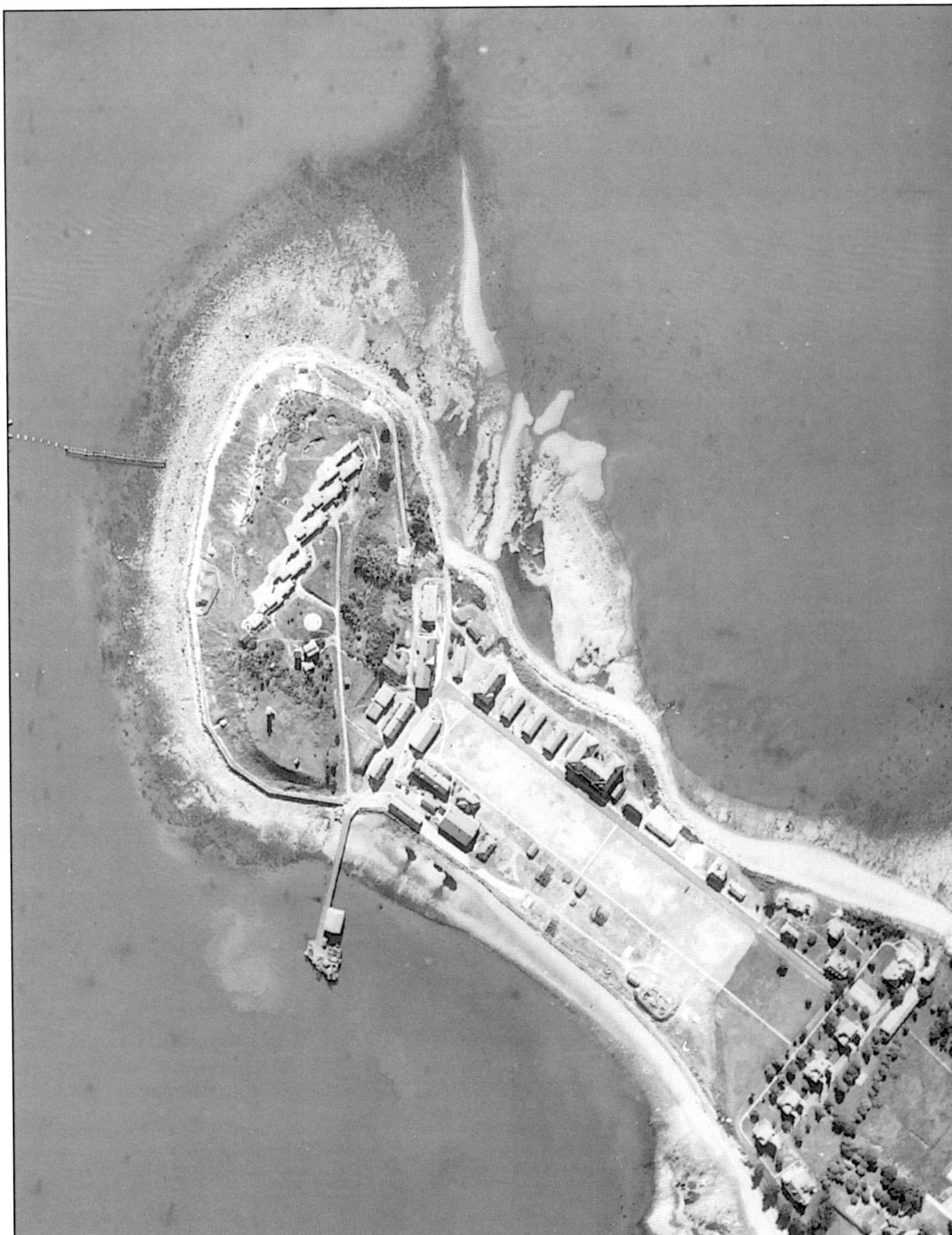

This June 1944 aerial photograph shows Fort Strong. Long Island Head can be seen in the upper segment of the image, while Officer's Row is in the lower segment.

Daily maintenance of the powerful 60-inch searchlights was vitally important. Members of the 9th Coast Artillery Regiment pose by their Fort Strong searchlight in July 1942.

A 3-inch antiaircraft gun in a sandbagged position at Fort Strong, 1942. The officer outside the sandbagged emplacement is Lt. Vahan Vartanian, who later became the adjutant general of Massachusetts.

For this soldier, it is winter guard duty at Battery Basinger with a 3-inch rapid-fire gun battery. In the background is the main channel. Fort Dawes is in the distance.

These soldiers practice their artillery drill on the 10-inch disappearing guns at Fort Strong. The soldiers are from Battery L, 241st Coast Artillery Regiment. By 1943, all of the major caliber guns were removed from Fort Strong, leaving only 3-inch rapid-fire and antiaircraft guns.

Responsible for mining the northern channel of Boston Harbor, Fort Strong shared both equipment and mine flotilla vessels. In this 1943 image, personnel from Fort Strong prepare cabling off the U.S. Army Mine Planter *Abbott*.

By 1944, both the northern and the southern minefields of Boston Harbor were equipped with the new ground mine. In this image, personnel of the 9th Coast Artillery Regiment aboard the mine planter prepare and align ground mine cables for rapid placement.

When a ground mine exploded, it caused a tremendous displacement of seawater, as shown by this remarkable image. This mine was activated as part of day phase practice on June 13, 1944, by Battery A, 9th Coast Artillery Regiment (Fort Strong).

Fort Strong soldiers aboard an L boat in 1943 tow out a target for mine practice. When the towing vessel began its practice run over the minefield, the towing cable was lengthened considerably.

Fort Standish, on Lovell's Island, became the "outpost" of Boston Harbor in 1940. The federalized national guardsmen lived in tents throughout their occupation. In this image, the soldiers on the island are very pleased to see the army transport arrive with mail.

Temporary wooden buildings and barracks were not completed for a year after the soldiers arrived at Fort Standish. The cool breezes of the summer months became blustery, snow-laden blizzards of winter that the soldiers endured, as this image indicates.

Construction of the temporary buildings began with deep foundations because of the sandy soil at Fort Standish. In this view, pipe trenches and water lines are being dug prior to the erection of the new buildings.

A formal retreat ceremony in 1941 occurs in the new barracks area of Fort Standish. By November 1942, all of the tents had been eliminated and the garrison lived in these T series wooden buildings that were standard throughout the continental United States.

Because of its isolated location, Fort Standish was important to the defense of both the northern and southern channels of Boston Harbor. In this image, a gun crew performs artillery drill on Battery Williams, a 3-inch rapid-fire gun battery.

A commercial ferry en route to Boston passes under the guns of Battery Williams. This channel is known as the Narrows. Fort Warren is visible in the background.

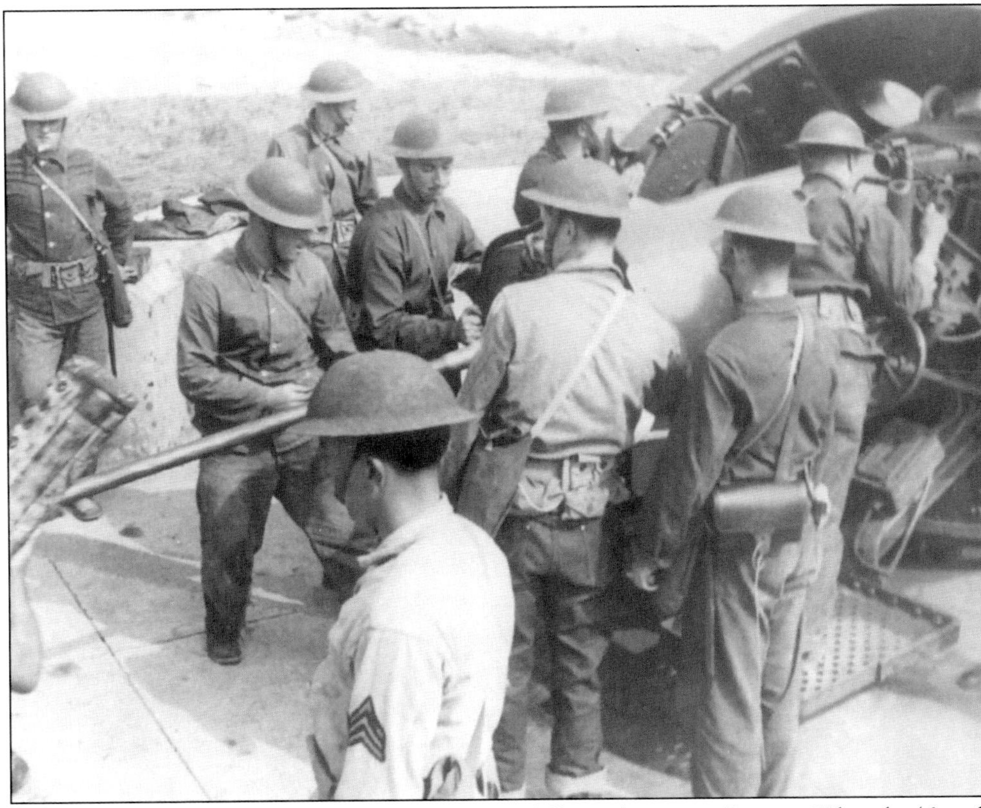

This gun drill simulates battle conditions with full combat gear: Battery Whipple (6-inch barbette) at Fort Standish, 1942. The projectile has just been rammed into the gun tube, and the powder bags (left) are about to be inserted.

Battery Whipple appears under camouflage netting and disruptive camouflage paint in 1944. Both 6-inch guns are visible under the netting, and the range-finding station to the right has also been camouflaged with a disruptive paint scheme.

This 1942 view of Battery Terrill shows a 6-inch disappearing gun battery, located at the northern tip of Fort Standish. This battery became outmoded; in 1943, a 90-millimeter anti-motor torpedo boat battery of two shielded guns was installed nearby.

Although all of the soldiers of the coast artillery were artillerymen first, the requirement that they also be infantrymen was never forgotten. In this image, soldiers at Fort Standish fire rifles on a known-distance (KD) range near the old lighthouse reservation.

In September 1940, federalized troops garrisoned Fort Andrews on Peddock's Island. The soldiers, composed from the 241st Coast Artillery Regiment, were quartered in the spacious brick barracks. In this image, sergeants are being inspected for guard mount.

In this view, the soldiers of the guard mount, clad in full combat gear, pose behind their barrack, following guard mount in March 1942.

Close order drill, under arms, were required for new trainees at Fort Andrews, *c.* 1942. The parade ground was kept immaculate, but during the day, it was in constant use by trainees learning the intricacies of marching and physical training (PT).

Artillery drill on the 12-inch mortars at Fort Andrews was very important in 1942. Mortar firings were coordinated with the northern mortar batteries at Fort Banks in Winthrop for concentrated fire upon a given target. By 1943, these weapons were obsolete.

A tremendous amount of teamwork and drill was required to fire 12-inch mortars because of the closed conditions of the firing pit and the nature of the weapon. The top image shows the breech being opened to receive the projectile and bags of powder, while the bottom photograph shows a mortar ready to be fired by the gun crew.

This view shows gun No. 1 of Battery McCook at Fort Andrews in 1944. In the upper photograph, the camouflage netting has been pulled aside to enable the gun crew to aim the gun as necessary. In the lower image, the entire camouflaged gun battery is visible. The odd-looking object in the foreground is an armored shield removed from one of the 3-inch rapid-fire gun carriages of Battery Bumpus, located to the far left.

When the weapons were removed from the mortar batteries, the filled pits served as excellent close-order drill areas for the soldiers. In this image, the soldiers are taking a cigarette break, while their rifles are in stacked arms.

Although not a coast artillery responsibility, naval net and boom obstructions were established at many channel openings in Boston Harbor during WWII. This segment, constructed to thwart motor patrol torpedo boats, stretched from Peddock's Island across Hull Gut. Fort Revere's standpipe is clearly visible to the right.

Six

World War II

Fort Revere, Fort Banks, Fort Heath, Fort Dawes, Fort Ruckman, East Point

In September 1940, Fort Revere was garrisoned by batteries of the 241st Coast Artillery Regiment. Temporary wooden buildings had not been completed at that time, and the soldiers lived in tents located in the old militia campground. Artillery and close order drill took place daily, as evidenced by these members of Headquarters and Headquarters Battery, 2nd Battalion, 241st Coast Artillery Regiment.

These two views show Fort Revere from atop the standpipe. The upper view looks toward Point Allerton, while the lower view looks toward Battery Ripley (12-inch barbette) and the new cantonment area.

This 1942 aerial view of Fort Revere shows the tremendous amount of reconfiguration being done to the landscape. The standpipe is in the upper mid-segment of the photograph. Battery Sanders (6-inch disappearing guns) is visible in the center of the image.

Fort Revere can be seen in this June 1944 aerial view. Notice that all of the gun emplacements are empty. All of the original weapons that remained at Fort Revere (Battery Ripley and Sanders) were salvaged by late 1943.

After 1943, ordnance that remained at Fort Revere were 3-inch antiaircraft guns and a 90-millimeter anti-motor torpedo boat battery. Other weapons, such as this sandbagged .50 caliber heavy machine gun, were positioned strategically throughout the fort.

Fort Banks housed many prewar supportive units for the harbor defenses that included offices for real estate, ordnance, and communications. After war was declared, countless civilians arrived to be processed into soldiers at Fort Banks. Numerous temporary buildings were quickly constructed at the fort, as shown by this 1941 image.

This 1944 view of Fort Banks shows most of the new temporary buildings. By 1942, over 70 new wooden buildings had been created at the Winthrop fort. By 1943, the Harbor Entrance Command Post (HECP) was constructed within a mortar battery magazine and served as the tactical bombproof nerve center for Boston Harbor.

In the upper image, 9th Coast Artillery Regiment soldiers perform an orchestrated artillery drill in the Fort Banks mortar pits in 1942. The lower photograph shows the plotting room of a 12-inch mortar battery at Fort Banks in 1942.

These two remarkable images show the 12-inch mortars being salvaged in place at Fort Banks. The upper photograph clearly shows the thickness of the mortar tube proper and the heavy castings and workings of the mortar carriage.

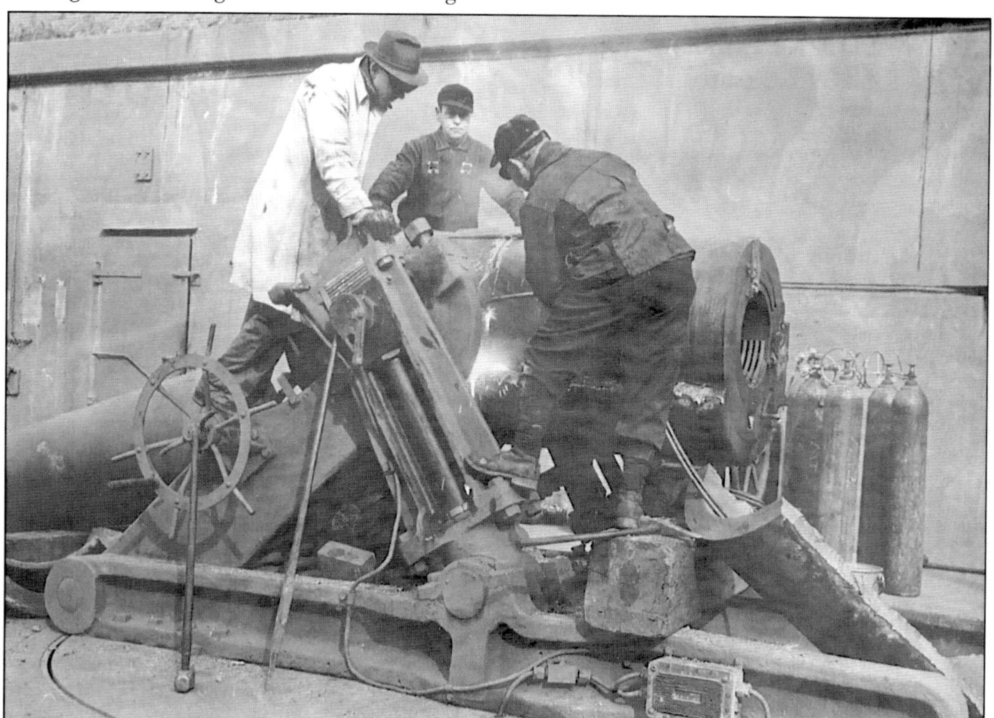

All supplies and personnel for the Harbor Defenses of Boston were shipped to Fort Banks and distributed from there. Many cargo trucks of varying sizes were required for this purpose, as evidenced by this 1944 motor pool image.

As modern seacoast gun batteries were completed and became operational by 1943, the intermediate, mobile 155-millimeter guns were transported back to Fort Banks for final disposition by the ordnance corps. In this image, 155-millimeter guns are stored in "artillery park."

In September 1940, Battery A of the 241st Coast Artillery Regiment was assigned to Fort Heath. Temporary buildings were constructed quickly at the small fort. As seen in these images, artillery drill was held daily on Battery Winthrop's three 12-inch guns.

Battery Winthrop at Fort Heath became an experimental battery for new methods of camouflage in 1941. Attempts to synthesize chlorophyll for camouflage nets proved unsuccessful, but the gun and battery net systems were adapted for coast defense purposes. In the upper image, the camouflage netting is shown at the rear of the battery, while the lower photograph shows a mock road over Battery Winthrop.

Two 155-millimeter guns were emplaced at Fort Heath in 1942 adjacent to Battery Winthrop. Camouflage and protection measures were elaborate, as can be seen in these two images of personnel placing sandbag walls and finalizing the emplacements.

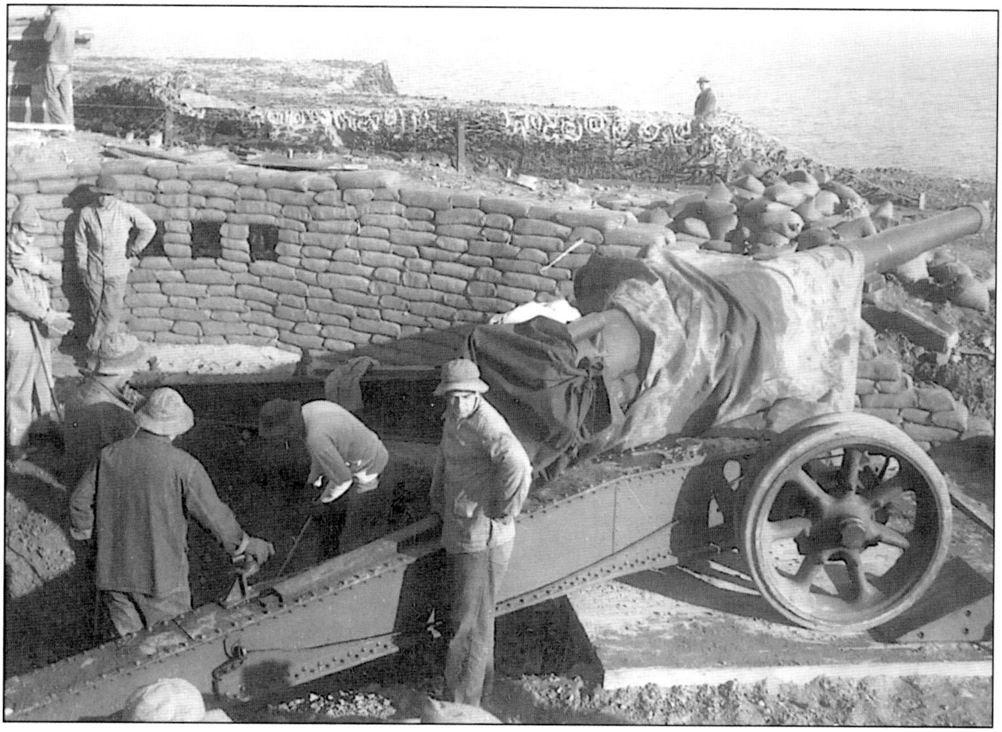

In September 1940, members of the 241st Coast Artillery Regiment garrisoned the Deer Island Military Reservation and were quartered in neat rows of tents near the center of the reservation. In January 1941, the reservation became designated Fort Dawes. By February 1941, two full-strength line batteries of the 9th Coast Artillery Regiment were assigned to garrison duty at the site and quartered in tents.

Prior to construction of the temporary buildings in spring 1941, the graves of Resthaven Cemetery had to be exhumed and the remains transferred to Fort Devens in Ayer for interment. Numerous, nonregistered remains were exhumed in the first two weeks. An investigation of City of Boston records determined that the nonregistered bodies were those of paupers who died during the influenza epidemics from 1918 to 1919.

In the upper photograph, workers construct the temporary buildings at Fort Dawes. Over the rooftops to the left of the new buildings, is the battle-damaged British battleship H.M.S. *Rodney*. In the lower image, the H.M.S. *Rodney* is docked at the Boston army base.

Fort Dawes was to receive the most modern seacoast defense systems that existed. Although the two massive guns were never mounted, the top view shows Battery 105, a 16-inch gun battery. The lower image shows gun room 1 of Battery 105 in 1944.

Fort Dawes also had a 6-inch gun battery (Battery 207). The two weapons were mounted in armored steel shields while ammunition, power, and plotting rooms were located in an underground, concrete casemate (bunker) between the guns. The gun tubes were never delivered to the gun battery, as shown in this photograph of gun No. 2.

All of the required ordnance, artillery, and signal corps material was installed in Battery 207. This photograph shows a diesel-electric power plant similar to that of Battery 207.

Fort Dawes also contained a modern mine casemate that controlled the north channel mines in conjunction with a secondary casemate (bunker), located on Great Brewster Island. This image shows the controlled mine panel boards at Fort Dawes in 1944.

In this 1945 image, the 90-millimeter anti-motor torpedo boat battery (at the tip of Fort Dawes) is visible, while a huge sign welcomes home servicemen returning from overseas duty.

The Harbor Entrance Control Post (HECP) was located at the highest hill at Fort Dawes and controlled every ship, whether military or commercial, that entered or departed Boston Harbor during WWII. In the upper image, the HECP shows a mixture of both army and navy manning personnel on the bridge of the structure. The lower photograph shows the HECP's busy interior observation bay in 1943.

The first soldiers to garrison Fort Ruckman in Nahant were from Battery C, 241st Coast Artillery Regiment. They quartered in tents, as shown in this *c.* 1940 image. Bayley's Hill and its observation station is shown near the top of the hill.

By 1942, Battery C had been transferred to Sagamore Hill, Cape Cod Canal. Members of two full-strength line batteries of the 9th Coast Artillery Regiment garrisoned Fort Ruckman and manned Battery Gardner, as shown by this *c.* 1942 photograph.

Battery Gardner was completely modernized and was camouflaged using extraordinary means that included mock roads and dummy buildings. The two 12-inch guns were casemated (covered over) against aerial attack and ship bombardment, while the interior chambers, such as the plotting and computer rooms, maintained gas-proofing systems. The 1944 upper image shows the entire battery, while the lower image shows gun No. 1.

Although Battery Gardner's new gun data computer and advanced electronic fire-control devices were installed in the plotting room, manual plotting equipment, as shown in this 1942 photograph, were retained for emergency use.

This 12-inch shell room was similar to Battery Gardner. The overhead rail system transported heavy shells from the magazine to the gun proper by a solitary artilleryman.

Fort Ruckman and Bayley's Hill appears in this *c.* 1945 photograph. Battery Gardner's exterior casemates are visible on the right.

Fort Ruckman also served as an overseas processing station and headquarters for the 143rd Mechanized Calvary Regiment. The calvary unit daily patrolled the northern New England coastline in jeeps, halftracks, and trucks in all weather and under all conditions.

The East Point Military Reservation at Nahant became active immediately following the attack on Pearl Harbor in December 1941. Two 155-millimeter guns were towed from Fort Banks, across Lynn Beach (as shown here), to East Point in order to protect Boston Harbor's northern approaches.

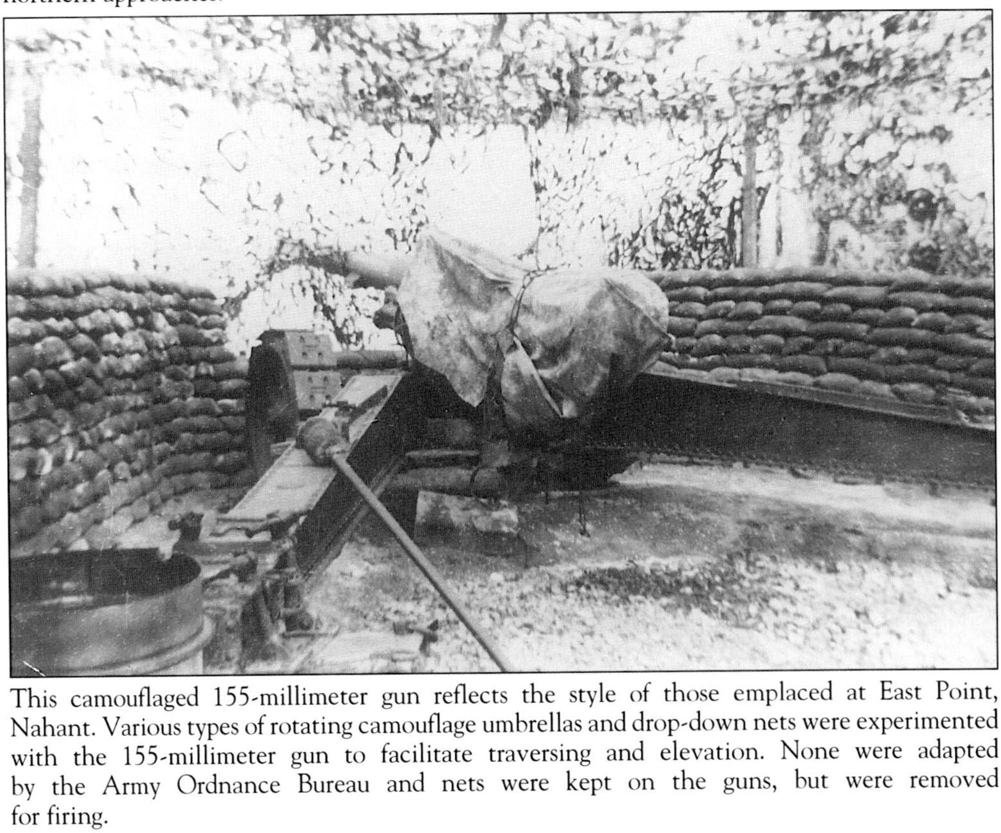

This camouflaged 155-millimeter gun reflects the style of those emplaced at East Point, Nahant. Various types of rotating camouflage umbrellas and drop-down nets were experimented with the 155-millimeter gun to facilitate traversing and elevation. None were adapted by the Army Ordnance Bureau and nets were kept on the guns, but were removed for firing.

The East Point Military Reservation appears in this 1943 photograph. The facility was to be named either Fort Oliver W. Holmes or Fort Henry C. Lodge, but neither name was approved by the U.S. War Department, and the reservation remained nameless throughout the war.

Headquarters for the East Point Military Reservation were inside the mansion at East Point and remained so throughout the entire WWII period. New installations were proposed for the reservation that included a naval magnetic loop station and modern 6- and 16-inch casemated gun batteries.

The smallest of the new gun batteries constructed at East Point, Nahant, was Battery 206, which contained two 6-inch guns in armored steel shields and an underground casemate (bunker) that contained plotting, ammunition, and power rooms.

This interior image of the plotting room shows a 6-inch gun battery of the style constructed in Boston Harbor during WWII. The sergeant is pointing at the plotting board on which a target's position was plotted from information fed in from distant observation stations and towers. This system was later supplemented with radar and computers.

The C.E. Hall Company delivered one of the 153-ton, 68-foot-long gun tubes to Battery 104 at the East Point Military Reservation in 1943.

The largest gun battery at East Point was Battery 104 (John B. Murphy). It contained two huge 16-inch guns in casemated gun rooms. Battery 104 was capable of firing a projectile that weighed over one ton a distance of nearly 30 miles. Gun No. 1 is shown in this 1944 image.

This overall view of Battery 104 (John B. Murphy) at the East Point Military Reservation was taken *c.* 1944. Gun No. 1 is to the left.

This remarkable image shows a 16-inch gun at the exact moment of firing a projectile. Identical to Battery 104, this photograph shows Battery 103 (Seaman) at Fort Dearborn, New Hampshire (Harbor Defenses of Portsmouth, New Hampshire).

Seven

World War II
Fort Duvall, Great Brewster, Outer Brewster, Calf Island, Fourth Cliff, Strawberry Point

In September 1940, Fort Duvall was garrisoned by Battery D, 241st Coast Artillery Regiment. The soldiers were quartered at Fort Andrews and Fort Revere until a causeway was erected in 1942. The huge 16-inch guns were fired in 1941, and the task of modernizing the emplacement and protecting the guns with overhead cover began.

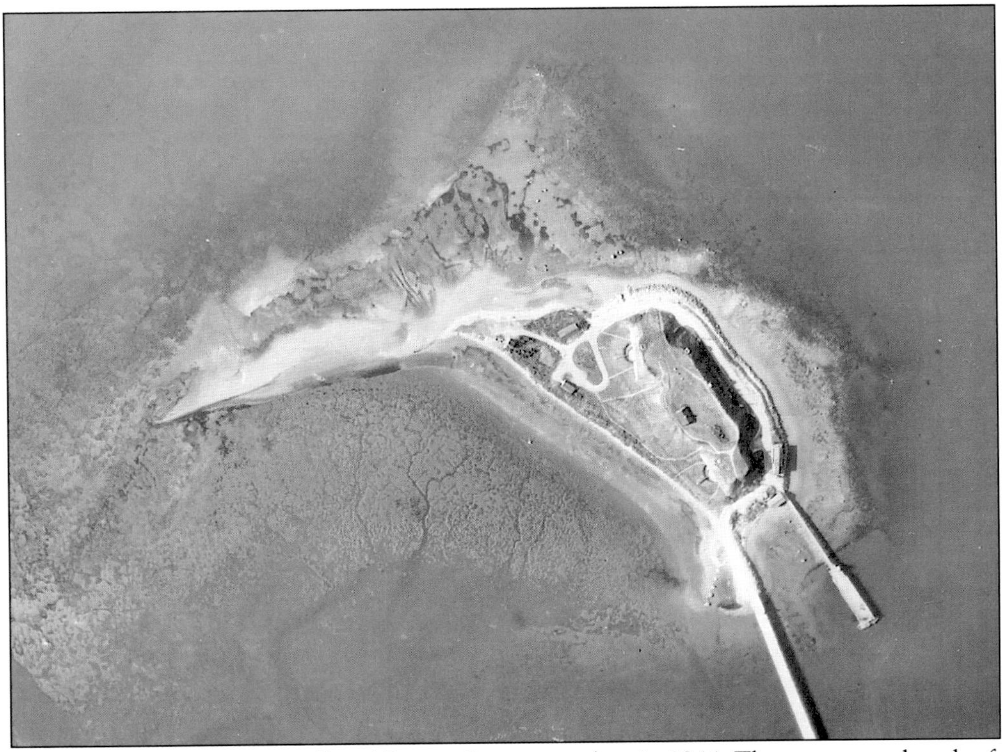

This aerial view of Fort Duvall and Battery Long was taken in 1944. The causeway, the wharf, and a small temporary barrack for the gun crew are visible on the right.

This 1944 view shows Battery Long at Fort Duvall after modernization. The small building atop the gun battery was a disguised observation station. The causeway is to the right.

The Great Brewster Military Reservation was created in 1941, but construction of the mine casemate, anti-motor torpedo boat battery, and temporary buildings did not begin until 1942. Great Brewster Island is shown from the landing approach, *c.* 1943.

Great Brewster's anti-motor torpedo boat battery consisted of two 90-millimeter shielded guns that were augmented with .50 caliber machine guns, as shown in this winter 1943 image.

Shown is artillery drill on the 90-millimeter anti-motor torpedo boat battery on Great Brewster Island in winter 1943. This dual purpose weapon could also be used against aircraft.

Additional weaponry on Great Brewster Military Reservation included 37-millimeter antiaircraft guns, as shown in this winter 1943 photograph. The reservation and all weapons systems were garrisoned by Battery C, 9th Coast Artillery Regiment.

The Outer Brewster Military Reservation was begun in 1942 and included a 6-inch shielded gun emplacement (Battery 209), three barracks and mess hall of reinforced concrete, a desalinization plant, and a long range radar installation (SCR-296A).

This front view shows Battery 209 on Great Brewster Military Reservation. The SCR-296A radar tower is visible to the rear and center of the gun battery. Battery 209 was unique, as it was named (Jewell) and it contained an interior protected water reservoir.

This image shows the tall, steel girder tower for the SCR-296A radar installation. Three additional prefabricated steel buildings for power and target tracking were established on the island for this unit. They were located between the three concrete structures for protection.

This 1943 image shows gun No. 1 of Battery 209 (Jewell) on Great Brewster Military Reservation. This remarkable photograph shows the shielded gun in detail as well as one of three entrances into the underground casemate (bunker).

The Calf Island Military Reservation was primarily used as an advanced antiaircraft searchlight and observation site from 1941 through 1943. Because of the abundance of wild rabbits on the island, the small garrison named the facility Bugs Bunny Island.

The garrison on Calf Island was composed of personnel from Fort Revere, on a rotating basis. When war was declared, the largest weapon on the island was a .30 caliber automatic rifle, which may explain this soldier's rather mournful expression.

In 1943, an SCR-268 radar, designated "bedspring" by operators, was brought to Calf Island for antiaircraft detection and searchlight directing. The top image shows the SCR-268 operating crew. The bottom photograph shows radar and searchlight units set up, ready for nighttime operation. By early 1944, this apparatus was obsolete, and the equipment was removed. The island was then abandoned by the harbor defenses.

The last static outpost of the Harbor Defenses of Boston was located at Fourth Cliff in Scituate. This unique installation, code-named Silver Sands, was constructed similar to beachfront cottages along the seacoast, while the 6-inch gun emplacement (Battery 208) maintained a mock road, netting, and small building for camouflage.

A 1944 seaward view of Battery 208, Fourth Cliff in Scituate, shows both 6-inch shielded guns and the underground casemate (bunker), containing magazines and plotting and power rooms. The white cottage hid the Battery Commander's Station in its basement.

Strawberry Point in Scituate (also known as the Glades) contained radar stations, observation stations, and a navy magnetic loop detection station. These images show two different styles of coast artillery observation and fire-control stations, *c.* 1943.

Eight

TERMINATION

Many of the coast artillery facilities in Boston Harbor were in caretaker status by late 1945. By late 1948, all but a few were surplus. By 1950, the U.S. Army had abolished all harbor defense commands and former coast artillery units were incorporated into field artillery or antiaircraft commands. During the Cold War, three former coast artillery sites—Fort Dawes, Fort Heath, and Fourth Cliff—were used for electronic experiments. Although all experiments were military in nature, the systems developed at Fort Dawes were later adapted into air traffic control. Those developed at Fourth Cliff, as the billboard array shown above depicts, were later used for scatter communications.

As new Cold War threats evolved, the requirement for missile defense increased. By 1956, Boston was ringed with 90-millimeter antiaircraft gun and Nike-Ajax missile batteries. Fort Duvall and Fort Ruckman were used as individual battery missile track and control sites. Fort Heath maintained a joint U.S. Army–Air Force system known as Missile Master. Fort Banks was headquarters for the missile batteries that surrounded Boston.

When the Nike Ajax missile batteries were phased out and Nike-Hercules systems were incorporated, only Fort Duvall remained active. By the early 1970s, the missile commands were eliminated and the forts were deactivated and abandoned.

Most of the forts are now parks, while some have been reused for commercial purposes. Of all of the forts in Boston Harbor, only Fourth Cliff has been retained by the military. It is now a U.S. Air Force recreation site for active and retired military personnel.

In this final image, the long-abandoned mortar battery at Fort Andrews on Peddock's Island captures the true essence of an abandoned military post.